EYELENS

EYE OF A MOVIE BUFF

ROHAN KOMPELLA

I would want to dedicate this work to my parents in order to increase their exposure to film as well as to myself in order to have a better grasp of the behind-the-scenes and scene-setting processes.

Contents

Preface — vii

Acknowledgements — ix

Prologue — xi

Lines That Impacted Me Learn About Cinema — xiii

1. Theatre — 1

2. Theatre Response And Euphoria — 5

3. Bgm Or Music — 8

4. Cuuuuuuuuuuuuuut — 12

5. Making Videos — 14

6. Camera Language — 17

7. Scene-to-scene — 19

8. Memes — 21

9. Second Show — 23

10. Genres — 25

11. Tragicomedy — 29

12. Does Movies Influence On Society? — 32

13. Mirroring — 35

14. Hit/flop — 38

15. Reviews And Critics — 41

16. Genre I Hate To Watch — 43

17. Fantasy, Fiction And Horror — 45

18. What If I Become A Film-director....?? — 49

Eyelens — 53

Preface

"We live the life of others when we read their thoughts....."

This sentence occasionally makes me believe that it is accurate. In my own level of context, from the time I was a baby to the time I was a young adult, it was always things like movies, novels, and music that inspired, motivated, and affected me to do many things regardless of right and wrong.

Beginning with my first film to a recent Netflix series, More than the academic teachings, I found myself wondering about the story, the characters, and life as viewed through their eyes. I firmly believe what I'm saying, despite the fact that there may be numerous and various reasons for this. The theatre encouraged me to study, acquire, and be motivated, in contrast to regular classes. I have always voiced my opinions on cinema, films, and movies. This book provides me with a platform to do so.

Films at times influenced my existence, my thoughts, and my actions over years, months, days, and even seconds at a time. This project, titled "Eyelens," consists of two elements. The first is that it is an expansion of my earlier work, "PLENTY THOUGHTS FROM AN EMPTY BRAIN," and the second is that it is a collection of my theories, ideas, and beliefs about movies, films, and how I compare them to my everyday life, turning them into serious fun.

*- **Rohan Kompella***

Acknowledgements

Regarding acknowledgments, I want to say how grateful I am to my father, who significantly influenced my passion in viewing and discovering new movies. The films dad tried to convince my brother and I to see as well as the many films he presented to us are what I respect above any other learning environment, and I remember every movie we watched together.

He introduced me to a wide range of genres, from indie films to Hollywood horror, that often catch people's interest. Whether it's a fantasy like Avatar, a catastrophe movie like 2012, a horror movie like "The conjuring," or even others that I might not recall now, but still it's his decisional aspect of letting us to explore us to the world cinema and the letting us in having access to various with the availability of interenet and devices .....

Prologue

Imagine being at a theatre with wide and various availability of audience where the trance of the cinema let them lose themselves and the environment with from celebrations to praising, praying and trance of devotion to cinema is something you never experienced ever before and the acts took place influenced and had an impact on you to know and learn about cinema and considering yourself as a lead character for your film.

Eyelens is the book with compilation of various thoughts, ideas, opinions and my consideration on cinema in life and life in cinema....

I many times considered from a situation to a conversation in terms of cinematic aspect which made me think and make out decisions, talk and considerations of any particular aspect...

Lines That Impacted Me Learn About Cinema

- "The cinema has no boundary; it is a ribbon of dream" .- Orson Welles,

- "Relating a person to the whole world: that is the meaning of cinema."- Andrei Tarkovsky,

- "Now more than ever we need to talk to each other, to listen to each other and understand how we see the world, and cinema is the best medium for doing this."- Martin Scorsese,

- "Cinema can fill in the empty spaces of your life and your loneliness." - Pedro Almodovar,

- "Cinema is the most beautiful fraud in the world." - Jean-Luc Godard,

- "Photography is truth...and cinema is truth 24 times a second." - Jean-Luc Godard,

- "I think cinema has this beautiful component. It's a universal language." - Paolo Sorrentino,

- "Cinema should make you forget you are sitting in a theater." - Roman Polanski,

- "I think cinema, movies, and magic have always been closely associated. The very earliest people who made film were magicians." Francis Ford Coppola,

CHAPTER ONE

Theatre

*I loved the movie theater,
so I always saw a lot of movies.*

- Ed O'Neill

After the hospital ward, where I was born and my house when I was a baby, the atmosphere I attracted to was the theatre. It was in 2004, when I actually had a experience of myself at a theate. I do remember my very first time entering a theatre with a large crowd around me.

The feelings of fear, curiosity, enthusiasm, etc., were still vividly remembered from frame to frame. I was curious about what was going on as the screen curtain rose with the sound of applause.

Then, the term "CINEMA" was projected, catching my whole attention, along with the virtual presence of people, characters, action sequences, a rainy environment, character's dialogues, and our collective laughter without a clear understanding of "What's happening.?", and

When I reflect back on the theatre experience I had that day, it was something that really stood out to me, and I started to consider a number of different concerns;

- What's the name of the location?
- Why are moviegoers enjoying the movie that is playing on the screen?
- How is the movie being displayed over there on the screen?
- How are movies made?
- Where was the term "CINEMA" created?
- Who is the maker of this thing we call cinema?
- Why are movies made?

One by one, these additional concerns kept me up all the night and punished me for being sleepy in class next day. The story of the movie, the characters we relate to, the high we experience during a high scene like the elevation for a lead characters, the tears that do fall from eyes without conscious control—all of these things inside it do happen without human consciousness, and that, in my opinion, is the theatre's ultimate power.

In addition to being a block and brick building with a limited number of seating options, the theatre also serves as a place where we go to explore our own kind and form of universe.

An investigation into the history of theatres and how they developed as venues for enjoyment and the expression of art took place somewhere throughout the course of a long period of time spent continuously viewing movies in theatres.

Aristotle's contribution to drama and theatre and the stories he developed in order to make the audience's connection to the story emotionally stronger rather than letting the people yawn while performing the story are all examples of the genres that went on to develop for an art to express, the classification and types of theatre being established from the earliest days of the 6th Century (BC) and the factors that helped the GENRES in terms of development and the consideration THREATRE RESPONSE is being discussed later on in the coming chapters.

I love to find myself where people lost themselves.....

On a personal level, I just view the theatre as a venue for artistic expression or narrative storytelling.

I went to my first movie alone in ninth grade, and I've continued to do so ever since. In addition to my regular moments with my parents, this was the first time I had ever watched a movie by myself, so I was a bit nervous and relaxed while I watch it.

From tranquil to pleasant, I found watching the movie with my family to be uncomfortable, so when I watched it alone, it was a completely different experience. I was able to visualise every scene clearly and let go of my fear of watching inappropriate videos. There may have been an underlying factor of intimacy between the characters to prove their relationship, but even so, I thoroughly enjoyed watching the entire movie.

I never think about my writing projects, academic classes I need to attend, examinations I need to take, or presentations I need to make when in a theatre. The distraction I encounter, the amusement I enjoy, and the tale or characters I connect with may be the cause, keeping me in the trance rather than allowing me to consider any other conditions or the implications I will need to confront after the movie.

I find watching a movie to be a pleasurable pastime, even if some people may find themselves in a 3-hour meditation to be a positive experience.

CHAPTER TWO

Theatre response and Euphoria

"I love to find myself where people lost themselves.."

Everything you experience in a theatre, from the time you enter, is entirely focused on you. The doors open early to give you enough time to use the restroom, select a seat, grab refreshments, and even read the programme that features a list of everyone who collaborated to make this event possible for you. If you purchased a ticket and are running late, they frequently postpone the play's start time for you. In order to prevent an actor, a costume, or a piece of furniture from blocking your view of the action on stage, director may seat in various seats throughout the theatre during rehearsals. The environment in this instance might be a live theatrical performance, but the topic at hand is the film theatrical experience.

While finding myself in holy placs with conducting activities like mass prayers, offerings, gatherings, praising the god etc.., which uphold their belief and devotion to the GOD in reference of considering him to the Almighty and ultimate powerful, it was then I found myself in theatre.

The whistles and the claps for thier choice of favourite lead characters, for thier dialougues, mannerisms, the fights between the protagonist and antagonist and for maybe many more..... leave them to loose themselves among the trance of the term CINEMA.. I do at times watch out theatre response in youtube so as to visualise the experience of audience to a particular film or to a scene which I might had missed in real-time.

The handling of every emotion with a particular sense and a capable nature of audience pulse is something driven by thoughts, ideas, and implementations of many; however, it's still that one single term people work for and get it done to a single product which, at times, makes it super hit and, at other times, the same effort or an extra effort implemented can make it a super disaster.

Theater serves as a prime illustration of *CONSUMERISM.*

Since the Ottoman era, the concept of responsiveness has been important when deciding whether to see a play or performance. Tragic plays were performed during religious festivals in Athens in the sixth century BCE, marking the beginning of Greek theatre. These in turn served as the basis for the Greek comic play subgenre. The two varieties of Greek play would become incredibly well-known, and performances would travel throughout the Mediterranean and have an impact on Hellenistic and Roman theatre.

The audience response and any of their act is something considered as vital for the play or performace to continue or either to stop the performance, if the audience didn't like it enough to show up, the performance could not go up and with the same reference to till date, the level of audience response is something considered to be the vital part in considering a film to be a hit or flop.

Euphoria

To express this context of material aspect I believe individual level of experience cannot make sense of make a grab of attention in learning the aspect of Euphoria.....I do remember the day watching a film with a wide range of audience and their response to the film, from the shouts to screams, claps, whistles, celebrations with papers flying onto screen of the theatre and etc., It's that celebration I consider at times powerful than any trance of any other powerful almighty....

How does this celebration does have a relation to the pure divine....?

I believe, trance of celebration of a cinema is equivaent to the devotion of god and trance of praying to god.

As of we consider some material aspect as god so as that we dress it up, decorate it with floors, we give it a home or a place to pray and praise, I consider the projection of cinema does have the same right and both the terrms here are cosnidered to tbe the entities prayed and praised.

- I saw people praying with tears in both the places,
- I saw people being in a trance of celebration in both the places,
- I saw people praising and

I had a view of audience in both the places with equal emotion and devotion...

BGM or Music

"Without music, life would be a mistake."
— *Friedrich Nietzsche*

Imagine walking in the rain while listening to instrumental background music that miraculously transforms the way you walk in the rain into a path through heaven. A selection of songs appropriate for the gym, background music, and other factors occasionally improve workout outcomes at times.

I do possess a fundamentally high capacity for observation, which can occasionally be more keen than the other senses. I have made advantage of this talent when and while being at the movies or at the theatre. The finale, in which the characters either die together or separately, has caused me to cry on occasion.

I logically believe that using MUSIC, is the purest form of emotion available in man made things, in this case used as background music, has the power to inspire or stimulate the brain to enjoy the things that do go around, to get inspired by the soundtrack of tough music for gyms or muscle builders, or to get moved by the final scene of the

Titanic or the death of Iron Man, among many other references, may cause a person's eyes to well up with tears.

"Music has the ability to transform any circumstance into something new."

Then, when a typical water fall was being filmed from a distance, and in addition background music was added, transforming it into something wonderful. Certain types of music does have the enough power to turn even the toughest individuals into sponges that have been immersed in water for some time.

I've always been intrigued about a film director's and a music director or composer's point of view as they build any kind of music or a genre of music while producing a scene or a film. After reading, talking to, and meeting numerous people online or in person with varied perspectives and understandings, I feel that MUISC and SOUND are two aspects that may be used to form the background of a movie.

Another branch of music theory is just how composers analyse the harmonic patterns of the music in movies, ranging from regional chord progressions to frameworks that span whole films; music's metric, rhythmic, and phrase forms, as well as its motivic and thematic elements, may influence how it connects to on-screen action or editing.

I believe that music is sometimes used to transmit an interpretation factor between the incident and the viewers or between the characters, to support the power of an emotion or any other thing, to uphold the power of feelings and emotions, whereas sound can be thought of as simply the BANG sound that hits the ears during the intro of a character or at times of scenes in a horror film.

Though sound is created by the brain, music is often developed from the heart.

I personally like Indian music director Ilayaraja's songs a lot, and there are movies where I watched a few specific scenes of his music with my eyes closed and my ears open. I did this simply to avoid the visual distraction and hear the music that carries and conveys the emotion of the plot or the characters.

I at many times listen to the background music than to the songs cause I personally connect to the music than to the lyrics and in consideration of facts there are songs where I concern to listen to the lyrics rather than the musical composition made and setup. It's my sensability and consideration factor in considering the term of what to hear and what to listen.

I believe that music has been an element of theatre performances for thousands of years. Since the tragedies and comedies of ancient Greece, music has played a significant role in Western theatre. Music might remark on the events taking place onstage, hint at a savage attack or a growing romance, or convey the deep emotional life of a character.

The six components of any drama are story, character, thinking, diction, music, and spectacle, according to the first theatrician, Aristotle.

The fundamental role of music in theatre is shared by other theatrical traditions from Asia, Africa, and other regions. Tom, the narrator, informs the audience as Tennessee William's play The Glass Menagerie begins: "In recollection everything appears to happen to music. That explains the fiddle waiting in the wings.

As a result of the same and numerous references, I approach BGMs on a very personal level. At times, I even relate to and feel connected by hearing to piano and violin instrumental music while and when thinking about something that took me off course and caused me to lose focus on my actual paths, as well as rock that is occasionally played for social movements and gym enthusiasts.

I never intended to think about music in terms of how it was made or composed or any of its technical aspects, but the final element that caught my attention and sent me into a trance made me realise that the way music is made and songs are written definitely plays a role in how something is meant to be understood as a whole. The basic goal of contemporary cinematic music is to be successful—to support the action and direct the audience's emotions. To do this, the composer employs common sequences and patterns present in all music to establish a solid foundation for them all.There are certain songs that I play often and that have words that are significant and have been composed in a way that is both comprehensible and catchy.

Music has always kept me motivated to explore, ponder, analyze, and write a lot, whether I was writing an essay for a test or a chapter for this book.

CHAPTER FOUR

Cuuuuuuuuuuuuuut

I recall the director shouting, "Cut!," as I happened to be there by chance.

I'm the type of person who carefully observes and considers everything that occurs in and around the environment I'm in, so I went to the shooting location to see a scene being shot. I overheard one of the assistants remark,

"The scene will be for approximately 1min long and train the actors with their separate dialougues and actions and answers," but then something unexpected happened, the director yelled for a CUT while filming the first part of the sequence.

I was struck by his response when someone remarked, ***"But...we didn't even complete our full dialougues...?"***

"I got what I wanted," the director exclaimed. A straightforward assertion with a nuanced meaning.

A CUT is a call to stop the action and signifies the conclusion of a take in cinematic terminology. The performer must continue acting and performing until the director commands "cut," otherwise they run the danger of ruining a beautiful shot. It is never the actor's responsibility to cease acting without the director calling "cut."

A movie's theatrical cut is the version that the production company or film crew has chosen to show in theatres. Producers or studios will occasionally, but not always, make their own edits to alter a director's vision. It does involve the removal or cutting of pointless and unnecessary sequences, the slow-paced and other phrases or scenes thought not required.

They may edit out sensuality, violence, or just simply trim movies for time, so they may broadcast more frequently.

As of the same, I soon began to understand the difference between the words "need" and "desire", I was impacted by a shooting scenario, which helped me to elevate my thoughts.

Never do we consider what we desire; always do we consider what we need. In relation to that, it also had an affect on my life; every want that was once a desire has now become a wish that is required; desires have been trimmed and morphed into needs.

I have always thought of this "CUT...!" mindset as allowing me to make decisions, think about ideas, and focus on what I need and want rather than on worthless desires which can ruin a beautiful scene of my life.

Making videos

I describe myself as a person with traits of strong observation, curiosity in things that are practically applied, and other things that typically capture my attention, to use a very simple phrase of in-built nature available for every human component... Similarly, or while I was doing and learning things, the phrase "making videos" suddenly entered my head as people around me began to consider and discuss it.

I used to believe that cinema was a ready-made genre and stage of entertainment that the audience could access via theatre displays or digital screens on their phones.

But what about the term in the background that truly contributed to creating the movie that we got to watch...?

The line "Behind every comfort we desire, there's a small sized battle" from a movie trailer that I saw and noticed actually inspired me to comprehend and understand what's actually behind everything made, and the curious aspect of learning how's the thing made and I still recall the moment that actually aided in the raising of this discussion.

"How is a movie made?"

The availability of the internet did play a role in enabling me to study about the technical features of a film for this inquiry of understanding. A conscious query arose from the inside material of my brain when I became conscious in terms of learning about items of cinema.

I used to read publications about filmmaking, including those about the camera and the script, as well as interviews with directors, cinematographers, authors about the plot, technicians, and others. All of these things influenced the way I think about and learn from movies.

I watch filmmaking videos to picture the "behind the screen" to "behind the scene" and the film director's explanation about his work, specifics of the FILM he worked for is something I compare to comprehend the film maker's idea and thoughts while developing the film....

The VFX breakdowns, Concept arts, the storyboards and etc cinematic terms or tools does intense my high while learning about a film and it's making process and progress.

I wonder the way the VFX being used in a film tough the actors or the technicians can just visualise it in the screen later, but it's the vision they work eventually for is the one I love about the work....As a result of having access to so much information about "behind the screen and scene" elements, I never actually watched a movie as a movie; instead, I may have begun to decipher how the shot names, camera choices, transitions, trailer cuts, cinematic storytelling, genre assumptions, and many other elements were meant to influence how I watched a movie.

Many people cautioned and questioned me about my interest in the films, advising me to watch them ON screen rather than observing them OFF screen to avoid being bored. I think you become more enthusiastic and euphoric when studying and understanding the terminologies used in the behind-the-scenes and beyond when you start seeing how things are truly manufactured.

I frequently compared the same scenario to real life in order to analyse the things that made me feel furious or any other emotion, as well as the same to the people around me, if I wanted to understand the cause of a character's rage in terms of a tale and its many elements.

Camera Language

Camera always stayed in the first place of "Curious things to know about" list.

"Camera language" isn't about the words and evolutionary words of kamera from latin or something else from somewhere, It's just about my experience of conscious usage of camera and my level-of understanding to the capture of camera.

In the very early days of understanding a camera, I used to have an application of the method "to click and to capture" but by the time I understood the real applicaion of a camera from an old sunday magazine does then took a wide and vast application from my level of application and understanding.

The camera has it's own-level of language in understanding and capturing the best and holding it forever. Whatever and whenever I watch a film, I love to look at the best and beautiful captures that are being possible by the work and art various hands together.

I consider camera to be a tool to show and to define a capture.

I do have a lot of interest to the camera and to film things as well. I may not perform it in terms of techincal lacks and relavant aspects but still, I always look at things with my eyes as camera of capture in a zoomout mode.

Does it mean any difference in capture with types of camera?

In a same year, I did had a watch a reginal film and in the same year I watched a bollywood film and in the same year I was meant to watch an hollywood film and I couldn't figure out the difference between the quality of films. It can be factors like my sensibility, understanding capacity of the quality of films.I think that most of the time, people struggle to understand how different camera outputs differ from one another. There may be a variation between a 20mm and a 200mm camera, but unless specifically taken into account, it is not something that should be estimated to the average person's sight in terms of qualifying a picture being taken.

CHAPTER SEVEN

Scene-to-Scene

I'm a Movie-buff, without any specific genre or selection preferences, but no matter what movie I see, I always try to pay close attention to what is occurring, and sometimes this careful observation has an influence on how I use what I see in real life.

Every time I deal with a situation, whether it be humorous or anything else with a serious format of genere, I refer to a movie clip. There have been times when I have used a situation in my life as an example of and comparison to a film.

To help explain, there is one incident that I would like to discuss to provide support for my claim of comparison to a movie. It was then when I had to make a visit a known-one at a hospital it was the corridor with a light focusing on the edge of the corrdor with the remaining filled with darkness, I felt like walking like a lead character from a random film who went to a hospital to watch his friend on the bed.

The walk in darkness towards the light can resemble the enlightning phrase of the character in terms of knowing apart from his expectation for "What happened..!".

Once I had a serious thought of "What are the elements that made a film go blockbuster and some other film go disaster...?", it was then once I observed an element or a phrase called scene-to-scene...

Similar to how I believe it's application in real-life term, any emotion of sadness or rage does need its necessity of existence just to the term of that particular scene. Continuing it to the duration of any other scene leads to skipping the movie.

Instead of staying in the same scene or idea the entire time, scene-to-scene transitions transport the spectator to a different period and viewpoint.

This was observed by me while watching a movie called FOREST GUMP very recent with my brother, the transition of scene-to-scene used is something I found interesting among many other films I have in my list. As of the same cinematic-rule, I always intended to use this SCENE-TO-SCENE format of life where and which I skip to the next seen as soon as the previous scene had it's expiry and never carried the thoughts, any material aspects further.

Memes

In its simplest form, a meme is any usually amusing picture, video, text, etc. that internet users quickly copy and disseminate. Often with little modification, memes spell out all the conceivable thoughts and the precise face they want to express to the world since they cannot have it exhibited 24/7.

I'm a memer, and I do make a number of memes based on happenings in my surroundings or when I'm with friends or family. On occasion, while I was with the same group of friends or family, the memes served as a counterpunch to their actions or a retort to whatever they had produced.

With the ability to watch different movies, I often relate the situations in my life to the scenes in those movies, and occasionally, while spending time with family and friends, I make a lot of memes with relevant movie clips or screenshots of scenes that are significant to my situation and use those to create or text relatable dialogue. I do recall the first meme I ever made and the options I used on both Instagram and WhatsApp with my limited understanding. It was only later, during the lockdown time in the 2020s, that I really mastered the use of the most fundamental tools accessible in terms of creating a meme.

A meme is developed and created in aspects of our everyday life application or reference of examples gathered, as well as our real-life term or phrase does have an allusion in view of developing a meme at times as well.

Memes frequently relate to our lives, and sometimes our lives do have relatable factors towards the memes. Indeed, MEME does have it's own theory to understand the concept and idea that is being hidden behind the meme in presentation or of image or video that replicates or imitates our lifestyle or the current and present situation at times,

The term "meme" was first used by Richard Dawkins in his 1976 best-seller The Selfish Gene. The term, which refers to an idea, behaviour, or style that spreads from one person to another within a culture, has since been appropriated by the internet can indeed be called imitation.

Through this process of copying, environmentally sensitive concepts and ideals have been incorporated into our cultural norms. The process of meme theory is demonstrated when someone acquires these environmentally concerned beliefs and duplicates them in their own way. As we can see, the advent of social media platforms has increased the effectiveness of imitation (as defined by meme theory). It is simple to claim that exchanging concepts like those in these instances can benefit our society or the environment. Therefore, it is clear that the meme theory may also describe movements like extremism when these beliefs are adopted and copied, which is again expedited by the use of social media.

CHAPTER NINE

Second show

**"To understand a film,
Prefer to go for a second show"**

The time of a day when I typically love to watch any movie is around the second showings.

Because at that specific time there's a more comfortable spot to view a movie. Assuming there will be a second showing allows me to envision the theatre in peace and continue enjoying the film till I pass out when I go to the cinema. This kind of seeing has always helped me to uncover a novel element in a cinematic aspect.

The peacefulness and unobtrusiveness of the stroll I take from the theatre to my bed after seeing a movie differs from the trance of the theatre I watched it in day.

Since and because there are negligible things that may be upsetting, the movie-going high lasts until you go to bed. Not only do I enjoy going to the movies in a theatre, but I also enjoy viewing movies at home on my laptop, tablet, or phone at night since, as I've already mentioned, the pauses are much more tolerable than they would be during the day.

Why do most people like binge-watching a Netflix movie or series and a Second Show at night?

There are many possible responses that cater to different sensibilities and individual levels of interest, but I believe that during the day, most people are intended to look after and take care of a variety of things depending on the list of tasks they need to complete, while the evenings and nights are something referred to as the end of a day so that there is a window of time to relax on the bed and watch a movie without feeling under any pressure.

Daytime brings with it a lot of activity, noise, hawkers selling goods near the house, maids entering, interruptions from neighbours, and other personal tasks, such as preparing and eating meals. Add misbehaving kids and their ongoing needs to this.

Nighttime signals the conclusion of the day, when there is less noise. Because everything around you is at rest, you can watch the movie without being distracted and clearly hear the conversation. Movies with a narrative, detective agents, ghosts, etc. become more captivating or spooky if watched in a room with just one low light and complete silence.

Genres

Everyday life involves a variety of genres in terms of the people we encounter, the conditions we face, the events we go through, and the repercussions of the movies we watch....

- From fiction to fantasy,
- Comedy to crime,
- Horror,
- Adventure,
- Mystery,
- Romantic,
- Drama and etc,

To consider the very first element of genre I always wondered the classification of genres with respective names and titles and tag considered.

Technically speaking, I define genre as a body of creative, musical, or literary works that have a common form, subject matter, or combination of these. A typical reaction to a commonly occurring rhetorical situation, genre has its own framework of form, whether it be artistic, commercial, with the evolution of a story, or anything else. Not all conventionality is uninteresting. Rather, it refers to a recognisable pattern for disseminating specific types of data to a designated audience as necessitated by repeating events.

Every problem has a solution, and you simply need to remember the formula before solving the problem, according to a quote from my favourite math teacher from grade 5. This clarified my whole doubt of classification of genres with respective to available types of cinematic or art based genre understanding.

The majority of **horror** films are founded on the premise that a cursed spirit or ghost is waiting to possess a young person. To attract viewers' attention and prevent them from being disoriented by their surroundings, they employ frightful visual effects and sound effects. Invented tales known as "horror stories" are written with the purpose of creating suspense and tension in a tale that is supposed to be frightful. This category includes tales including ghosts, vampires, witches, or werewolves. There is typically a development of demented or dark traits as well as fear and shock.

With reference to numerous blogs, articles, and explanations where I understood that an **ACTION-FICTION** has the same central dilemma: How do I defeat powerful outside forces out to destroy me and other innocent victims?, I learned that an action-adventure can have its own formula, mandating players to undertake some sort of action in order to obtain a valuable item like a diamond, treasure, or anything else.

An action story's overarching theme or Central Theme is: When the protagonist makes a sacrifice to defeat or outsmart their exterior and internal opponents, life is preserved. But when the main character lacks the guts to make a sacrifice for the sake of others and themselves, death ensues.

A **Science-fiction** story may be created with the necessity to conduct an experiment, whether it involves time travel or superhuman feats of strength.

I take Spiderman as an instance to define or illustrate fantasy. A distinguishing feature of fantasy is the author's inclusion of narrative elements that aren't completely reliant on antiquity or the natural world for their coherence. My friend and I used to try to get stung by a spider in the initial days of watching Spider-Man to make sure we didn't end on the list of individuals who are Spidermans. Realistic fiction, as opposed to fantasy, is exempt from having to account for reality's natural laws and historical development. With reference to book named "Rhetorics of Fantasy" by Farah Mendlesohn. The states that the four kinds of fantasy proposed by Mendlesohn—portal-quest, immersive, incursion, and liminal—come from the protagonist's interaction with the fantastical realm. Mendlesohn makes the case using these sets that the categorical demands that author chooses to write in ultimately define their aesthetic choices.

A disastrous picture or disaster movie is a type of movie that uses a disaster as the main theme or story mechanism. Natural disasters, accidents, terrorist attacks, and pandemics are a few examples of such tragedies. A natural diasater or a survival concepts like zombieland and films give me a high of considering all the possible acts after a natural calamity to occur and I even at times figured out in terms of persoanl-level of survival to make sure to be alive in case of any act or event to occur. I watch these kinds of survival films after choosing horror films, whether they are based on natural disasters, pandemics like the zombie virus, or any other kind. I thoroughly enjoy it and I pay close attention to them while focusing all of my attention.

I tend to watch films of various genres cause I believe each genre has it's own flavour of taste in terms of cinematic exposure and experience and I always seeked to have the experience and exposure towards the various and vast available.

CHAPTER ELEVEN

Tragicomedy

In a very basic structure or mean of defining what's a TRAGICOMEDY is..... A literary technique called a tragicomedy is employed in fiction. It features both comedy and tragedy. Usually, the characters in tragicomedy are exaggerated, and sometimes there could be a happy ending after a sequence of bad occurrences. It is interspersed with jokes throughout the tale, merely to lighten the tone.

There exist few particular scenes at times while watching either in TV or while watching any film, there exists few scenes or clips where the humour is generated out of serious situations.... Any humour we laugh at is basically the counter dialougue or the consideration we consider from serious aspect of a situation.

I do remeber, the very early times of knwoing about this while reading a random article and it was then in FRANCE in the late sixteenth and days of early seventeenth centuries is the tragicomedy is the "BAROQUE". In usual reference, "BAROQUE" is used in reference to other art forms as well in music, sculputre and etc art forms.

Although different types of musical compositions and consequently different "styles" were developed during the 200-year period, the basic baroque characteristic which remains constant. BAROQUE music is polyphonic, containing many "voices"- a BAROQUE characteristic which occurs in literature as well.

Most of the research has found largely on English and German manifestations of tragicomedy, but no definitive theory of it has emerged, it's specific nature has not been determined. In terms of specific, existing and present researches does not address the problem of the specificity of tragicomedy but rather most often bases it's identification either on the oxymoronic nature of the name-concluding that tragicomedy is a mixture of the name- concluding that tragicomedy is a mixture of two genres tragedy and comedy, on the subject matter or on it's denouement- identifying tragicomedy as a tragedy which ends well.

The rigid separation between tragedy and comedy that is supported by the Aristotelian paradigm then in vogue in France makes the idea that tragicomedy is a combination of tragedy and comedy all the more startling. Most theorists of the sixteenth and seventeenth centuries, following Aristotle, emphasised this division by highlighting the distinctions and, in most cases, oppositions between TRAGEDY and COMEDY, such as the types of characters unique to each: noble, high-born characters of tragedy; common, low-born characters of comedy.

The tragic figure must, in accordance with the Aristotelian paradigm, be neither nice nor bad but rather someone the audience can empathise with—someone whose misery is not caused by any sin but by poor judgement.

This condition makes the audience feel empathy for the "undeserved misfortune" and dread since (s)/he is similar to the observer, and this "catharsis" is what makes tragedy effective. This catharsis is a natural result of the actions that lead up to the climax where it occurs.

The conversations we have and the humour we experience are examples of how we live in a TRAGICOMEDY-filled world. In my life, I categorised every conceivable element, scenario, and result under the category of humour.

Serious aspects of life are where humour originates, and tragedy plays a role in the development of comedy.

Doesn't make it worthless in considering everything comedy or under humor?

The moment you take everything serious you cannot even enjoy your company to yoouself too. I intend to believe there's a pretening nature in the humans. They pretend busy, they pretend serious, they pretend innocent and many other considerable pretending factors that assist them to live in a pretending world.

In personal matter, I enjoy a very serious situation in a humourous aspect of life so as that I take them to whole level conisdered since they make me smile and laugh. When you cannot make a humour out of any aspect of feel or emotion you didn't actually understood the feels and the emotions.

CHAPTER TWELVE

Does MOVIES influence on society?

DOES MOVIES INFLUENCE ON SOCIETY ?

This question can be generated either by a fool or either by a genius ....

"Children's brains are greatly impacted by film, and young people are influenced to imitate criminal behaviour. Personally, I think that CINEMA should be outlawed completely so that the future may be better with inventions and ideas than this garbage." While browsing through some strange trends on Twitter, this line caught my eye.

Cinema will always have an important role to play in society.

- Leslie Caron

Movies influence on society and individual's actions caused crimes to happen, rapes to take place and many other things to take place is something a war of debate from ages....I believe, restricting a entertainment source of entity and assest and considering a BAN or boycott can make society a better place to live is the idea of an idiot....

I believe, Cinema is an art form of telling stories in each and individual style of film making techniques.

From natural disaster films like 2012 to Sci-Fic like Avengers or Avatar, Action-drama, suspense-thrillers, murder-mysteries and etc is to say a story of characters and leads with which they have faced any determined situation are considered to be for entertainment purpose rather then influencing a man to be THANOS......and the crime that took place in any scene of a film does have it's considerable factors like story and emotion that influenced the main lead or the hero to take a necessary action or path called VIOLENCE.

Many studies by many releaved that,

"If movies have an influence on things like SOCIETY in real life,

I suppose real-life term like SOCIETY does have it's affect on movies."

I once heard a friend of mine say that watching violent or illegal acts on screen can lead a man to follow those paths. I believe and somewhat agree with this statement, but I still think that considering or blaming a movie in terms of criminal activity requires careful thought and consideration of the human brain.

For instance, any relevant conduct that resembles an intercourse is something that people deem embarrassing because an intercourse circumstance is meant to reveal the intimacy between the characters rather than having them for no use.

The environment that a person chose to live in and around is the explanation for this, in addition to that, Karl Marx once observed that a man is made by his circumstances. As a result, there are many and varied aspects to take into account in order to comprehend and support views of the effect of film on society.

Every aspect, term, entity, assest or any form is a COIN and it does have it's face known and unknown or positive and dark side to know and to explore.

CHAPTER THIRTEEN

Mirroring

In order to occasionally feel as like I was having the same heroic degree of experience, I used to replicate the motions of characters from movies I had previously watched and admired.

Here, I think that individuals often mimic or act in the same way as their most recent movie because of the beliefs they are related to. We can relate to fictional characters' stories due to our meaningful interactions with actual people throughout our lives. We virtually always sense empathy and compassion in our interactions with people, and they are important factors in how we react to fictional characters.

Few characters to hate is love the hatred and few characters do have it's hand in terms of considered a hate to love. Any character appreciated in a movie is something that tends to be created with specific aspects of making it too marketable.

The villain's character is created with the intention of making people despise it with terms like selfish, violent, and does have a lot of desires in terms of vanity, whereas the protagonist's character is designed with the purpose of having people really love it with concepts such as liberal and conditions, as of the master-slave morality, the liberal, humble, common, and another few terms are considered to be GOOD part and term loved by the majority of people.

As a result, people generally adore and admire heroic characters who do good and despise villains who cause harm, according to sociological theories of good and evil. The majority of the time, in terms of interpretations, I think it's the expanding human factor that causes him or her to acquire things from the environment around them. These specific factors can be described as his level of sensibility and thinking abilities that cause him to conceive the idea of adopting a characteristic from things that do go around him.

Even with the help of self-examine or self-analysis and observation, we does this act of adopting a character with the film we watched 10 seconds ago and walk out the theatre with the same mannerism and thoughts of the character we loved. Any medium is clearly essential to any communication since it both creates and conveys the messages that make up the process itself. It doesn't matter if one's primary emphasis is on communicators or viewers; the medium itself and its content always demand attention.

As a result, both direct and recorded reports of the abuses of a production process and inferences from of the films themselves serve as the foundation for the widespread view that cinema economic system devalues creativity.

Even the "effects" argument is made using abstracted movie material and self-declared claims of influence. What movies say and how they express it are vital if we are to start understanding the structures of modern civilization. Cultural meaning is important. The findings show how movies affect viewers' attitudes, prejudices, and opinions. Movies may dramatically change racial and gender stereotypes, attitudes toward certain groups of people, and lead to the development of fresh perspectives on a range of issues.

Finding a clear answer to the question of how effective mass media is and identifying a single method in which it affects the human psychology and behaviour appear to be difficult tasks.

CHAPTER FOURTEEN

Hit/Flop

When a movie is released, we frequently hear the phrases "Hit," "Superhit," "Blockbuster," and "Average," "Flop," and "Disaster." I believe the words "HIT" and "FLOP" reflect the contrast between the decision-making and considerational aspects of both the film-technicians and the public.

It may be any film with a lot of technical work and input in the script, screenplay, editing, action scenes, and many other areas, but it still stands out in the market as a DISASTER, or it can be different film with enough technical aspects and stand out as a BLOCKBUSTER.

A movie is basically a telling of a tale that revolves on characters and leads and the consequences they must deal with depending on the circumstances.

In a genrealised category, A HIT MOVIE is anything that may be categorised as a movie that the audience loved. A FLOP MOVIE is one that received a lot of criticism from the audience for being disliked and despised. I believe the audience can be compared to the five fingers we have at our disposal, each of which has a different range of heights and sizes. Some people enjoy watching romantic genres, while others detest crime and violence; there are differences in the senseabilities that come with audience availability.

I frequently watched flops more often than hits in this context, up until the point where I personally stopped watching it because, like up until the point where I personally find it to be a headache, I did observe every cinematic element, hazard a guess at the terms used behind the scenes, and watch a movie in order to distinguish between all the different factors that could have turned one into a blockbuster and left the other in the lurch of disaster.

If it can be a film like PSYCHO (1960) which stood as a mark for psychopathic films and it can be a film like RICH AND STRANGE with the lowest reviews awarded. Here the case to be considered is that both the films are directed by one man alone named ALFRED HITCHCOCK.

If a director like ALFRED HITCHCOCK can make a movie like PSYCHO based on the mental capabilities and concerns of a youngster who lost his mother and the thoughts of her personality prevalent within him and the thought process that instantly change with scene to scene. Just the period of time spent deliberating or choosing, regardless of the outcome, comes into focus afterwards.

Movies can fail for a variety of causes and succeed for the same ones.

The only certainty is that a movie requires time and a strategy to attract an audience if it is to recover from a failure. Although it may seem obvious, it was challenging to watch classic films from the previous, whether they had been hits or flops, before the invention of television and home video players and I do think that a movie takes longer to become recognised the more creative it is.

I personally thought about a lot of my actions and decisions in terms of whether they would be deemed a hit or a flop, which is an intriguing way to think about movies. In this situation, the majority of my decisions have been hits while several have been flops. So who exactly am I....?

Why would I make a decision if I knew for sure that it would be a mistake?

and why wouldn't I choose it if I knew it might have a major impact?

I used to compose short tales based on several genres that I found interesting. Of the remaining pieces, one in particular received a lot of reader recognition, and very few of them were skipped. Why would I create anything that take a SKIP into account, and also how did I realize a script would be well received by readers?

This decisional aspect need not exist and carry over to the subsequent ones; it may alter depending on the material that is accessible and the decisional elements of the individual with all of his worries for things to establish or to do so....

The point is now that each and every single one of us is only as excellent or as horrible as the stuff we choose to study at the moment and of how our lives develop from there. Fair enough, the stuff I or anybody else picks up is an individual choice, but without understanding what variables caused that choice at that specific time, one cannot take it for granted that someone is either incredibly brilliant or has lost it.

CHAPTER FIFTEEN

Reviews and Critics

"To avoid criticism say nothing, do nothing, be nothing."

— Aristotle

Reviews of a movie are something that audiences and watchers do consider and watch as soon as a movie is out and before going to a movie.

I used to like and refer to the remarks made by the reviewers and critics before deciding to see the movie at very early stages of comprehending a review or what a critic performs in terms of his job-role.

But later, after going through a lot of experiences and worries, I recognised that my own experiences really made a difference with his opinion of the movie, and I stopped looking back at the reviews.

The reason I never read the reviews again is because I realised that every person has a different level of film sensitivities. For example, someone who experienced bullying in school will find it upsetting to see it depicted on screen and will consider it to be an emotional trigger.

Violence and graphic details like blood will also make some viewers dislike a film.

I often think of a film's language in terms of scenes one after another or the story's foundational elements coming together such that the characters had a history that motivated them to take up a knife and pursue the way of walk to the violence.

I had undergone many reviews or listened to many critics to thier point of views of the film but never heard of the understanding element of considering possible factors that made the character to pick-up the point of violence and factors.

CHAPTER SIXTEEN

Genre I hate to watch

My exposure to and familiarity with virtually all film genres came close, but there is one that I avoid viewing: the love/romantic genre. To be honest, family dramas and romantic comedies make me feel more irritated and unreasonable when I consider looking at or watching them. Even if I may not remember the last movie I saw in that genre, it has been quite lot longer since I have seen a romantic movie.

This isn't just about me; according to many survey, many individuals dislike looking at and watching romantic films.

The potential causes, which I personally understand, are the absence of reality in most movies.
Too ODD or too much love tends to make people dislike it, but there may be many other reasons as well, such as the erroneous sort of viewpoint a select few had formed, the amount of meaningless material individuals occasionally faced when watching, and maybe many more.

I do occasionally receive a lot of criticism and praise from my friends who does ask, how I can classify myself as someone who is generally excited about learning without having viewed or seen a movie in that genre.
Although I felt this was a lovely question, the observatory aspect meant for my thoughts to despise it rather than for

me to at least change myself to view it.

The inclusion of pointing guns towards each other under the table with no one noticing and then with a cunning and husky mix face is something I prefer to watch and look at because I find the typical coffee scene with hours of looking each other over and discussing things of personal contexts to be extremely boring.

I feel Rom-Coms or pure dramatic films and the romatic genres have no sense in terms of existence. Because if it's the characters that deploy an emotion with words and tears I feel it's manipulation.

To convey your thoughts I feel one must term them in application of act rather than head shake for an acceptance to rejection.

CHAPTER SEVENTEEN

Fantasy, Fiction and HORROR

I enjoy watching fantasy and fiction movies with a mix of action and adventure, genuine or fabricated mysteries, since it broadens my viewing experience rather to just gazing at and listening to uninteresting dialogues between two people in a coffee shop or on a phone call. In my very early years, the fantasy films that heightened my viewing experience were HARRY POTTER, SPIDERMAN, MUMMY, and JURRASIC PARK, with extra and supportive aspects of my father who literally opened up the doors of the borders in regards of cinamtic exposure.

He allowed us to see movies with advanced technical aspects of filmmaking and the production process, making them extremely similar to the realistic experience of a picture. This helped me to increase my comprehension level from watching regional or highly popular movies.

In order to prepare myself with reference to movies, I repeatedly thought about a forthcoming circumstance with 2-3 or even more potential aspects while keeping in mind the purpose of fantasy and fiction. When I'm waiting, I watch what's going on around me with a cinematic eye, attempting to predict what may happen in the very next scene.

I do recall a humorous incident that I once predicted with my friends while waiting in a waiting room where I saw someone else gathering necessary documents to hand over to someone higher-official and at the same time there was the entry of the positional person with a distracting phone call and I forecast a splash between the two with my friends and they predicted the opposite to happen and the walks between the both in step by step was something I and my friends went interested in and it therefore resulted in my prediction to win.

As of this, in consideration at many times, I considered situations of real in terms of predicting it to happen with reference to movie-scene and in replication to it too.

Even while I may not be able to explain why this occurs, I do have some theories as to why it would occur in the first place when comparing actual occurrences to fictional ones.

I find real-life aspects to be a boring because while watching a film the scene and film does skip off the every building block of the story and in end we tend to see it in a zoom out and out-focused ones, whereas in real life terms we are tend to face it and we need to wait up for all the blocks to be placed one after the one, here my considerable role of making it from boring to interesting is that, I consider that particular situation of circumstance to the level of a film-clip or the plot I intended to develop.

It was once on my birthday and I was awake and watching a horror movie with such a wet and windy climate beyond my room and the howling sound and stormy noise from outside the window intensified my viewing experience inside, and at that point the establishing shots of the building and the room where the ghost exists had been that was when a sudden scream with a zoom-out left me in feel of fear and when the screen went out, because I was watching it at night and was in a dark room, I felt frightened. The child's cry of terror also contributed to my feeling of fear..

"If movies are the dreams of the mass culture...
horror movies are the nightmares"
- Stephen King

Horror everytime remained in the initial place of my interesting plot of genre both on and off the screen. I always preffered this particular genere from the remaining genres that I like to watch and hate to look and I remember the line which states that "In the absence of love, evil thrives".

When I actually read many of the film-technical articles regarding the horror film-making I observed many elemts that ended-up in experiencing them in the end of my street which does have an old-house left abandoned and my room with a minimal lighting that enters inside and the shade of shadow I do experienced at the corners of the room, is it all about my illusionary view or maight be true or the fictional imagination I do at times consider in existence.

The difference can be termed here is that, Illusions often include perception and cognition, while fantasies and imaginations focus on a different scenario or events that may happen in a different, worse-case scenario.

The RAAT and The Conjuring are the two types of films with one in category of . The Conjuring was the first Hollywood horror movie I saw with a lot of jump scares after seeing regional horrors.

The sounds I hear at the highest degree of experience include the creaks of old doors, walking sounds, wind noise levels, the sound of fabric blowing in the wind, the unexpected splashing of water valves, as well as the stromy gusts of trees leaning on the house and other objects.

CHAPTER EIGHTEEN

What if I become a Film-director....??

This question does have a backstory and preface in view of consideration and a raise in my brain...

Then, as I was describing to my companions all of the technical possibilities, one of them asked me in a serious tone, "Why don't you try out being or becoming a director...?"

A very common question that was asked in a very common way struck my thoughts in an unusual way.

I began to consider all the reasons why and how the query actually arose.

Does he mean it honestly? or maybe just some normal, casual humour...

Did he ask me this question in an effort to hear my response? and many other questions.

My curiosity in viewing a movie and learning about them has been piqued by these and other other topics that have been addressed around self-examination.

In order to make everything more fascinating and relevant to the sort of observatory, I always had this thought process and decision-making process where I examine a WHAT IF? scenario. This allows me to contemplate something from the ordinary to the extraordinary. I think about the idea of visualisation in filmmaking in light of a quotation from Picasso, who famously said, "Everything you imagine is real." Similar to how the mental image I have in my head needs several possibilities to help people understand my tale,

I decided to watch every director interview I could find in order to learn about their perspectives and justifications for their movies. After trying to study a lot and reading books like SHOOT LIKE TARENTINO and SHOOT LIKE SPIELBERG and many other books, I even once kept notes in my phone to remember all the potential film-making points and things discussed by them while watching the interviews, but I never actually had a note to maintain. I believe they just got in my thoughts.

Even when I watch interviews, I can answer the question presented by the interviewer on the director's behalf using his or her typical modes of reasoning and level-appropriate explanation.

Regarding movies, I have a few favourite subgenres, my own approach to cinematic narrative, and a target I always want to hit: the best outcome with the fewest technical demands.

I tend to integrate knowledge about language, vocabulary, formulae, techniques to writing stories, narrations, concepts, and many other aspects of filmmaking within myself to help me improve my cinematic manner and style of story telling through the medium of cinema.

The interest of one's own level of understanding a film can always help him to make a film.

Is it about the term HIT/FLOP?

A hit or a failure, as stated before in this book, doesn't, in my opinion, exist at the human and situational level of decision-making. Instead of the person who had his own format of work in creating the film from a piece of paper to a screen, it may have its term and name after having a broad recognition from sources like audience response and the box office term of financial aspect and such.

The phrase "it's never about the term of making the faults or avoiding the defects in my work" is stated somewhere in this book. Everything revolves around the material component I valued at the time and the external or internal influences that affected whether I thought my action was sensible or dumb. I would

The Stories I want and wish to say......

I always had this query in my brain in terms of understanding my own level of what to say and what to make to tell my story.... and ages later I figured few concepts and genres to say a story in terms of film-making are the, POWERFUL characters of Mythlogical and from Historical and at times it can be the characters I want to implement in the present societial element with reference of characters existed ages before, the sci-fi themes in my story and the action-adventure with the element of discovering treasure can be fantastical, but they have always been my favourite themes in my writings and developments. The unsettling component of my character arc with a fantasy story in a time and place of pandemics like the zombie virus, natural calamities, and survival concept also excites me to enjoy and improve my perspective of cinematic aspect.

I do enjoy tales and movies when it relates to HEROIC content and movie genres. I've always appreciated how the plot of the story, also known as the monomyth, is a common framework discovered in storytelling theory and comparative mythology. I also enjoy how the character is elevated for glory and how the plot that develops around the figure in both portions of cinematic storytelling. It refers to tales in which a hero leaves on an adventure, survives a life-or-death situation, and then changes or is transformed upon returning home.

Eyelens

The reason for considering the title EyeLens is that, the Camera and term Cinema had an effective influence on my observation and viewing very simple terms of daily-life into some kind of dramtic consideration and this enhanced my level of fantasical imagination. The eye catches pictures similarly to how the camera does, therefore the two have a lot more in similarity than merely intellectual philosophy. Contrary to popular belief, the camera's anatomy has more features in common with a real eyeball, such as a cornea that resembles a lens and a retina that resembles a film.

So the camera from it's intial stage of being developed had an influence from eyes in terms of viewing and capturing the moments and the term cinema is again filmed using the same camera. So in view of a title that tends to stand as a FIGURATIVE and METAPHOR, it was then the word EyeLens was hand-picked from a possible titles of 75 I thought of.

This book is a compilation of the ideas I've collected and been inspired by while studying and conducting research by viewing movies and reading books about movies. The opinions and viewpoints I formed while observing them, along with the fantastical ideas I conjured up from the very ordinary things that actually happened around me, helped me turn the mundane things I was looking at into interesting factors that turned the ordinary things into the extraordinary.